IN THIS PROUD LAND

Roy Emerson Stryker now lives in Grand Junction, Colorado, not far from where he was raised. After teaching economics at Columbia University, where he first became aware of photography as a powerful aid to social reform, he went to Washington, D.C. After producing the remarkable collection of photographs for the FSA, he went on to establish another famous one for Standard Oil. The publication of *In This Proud Land* coincides with the year of his eightieth birthday.

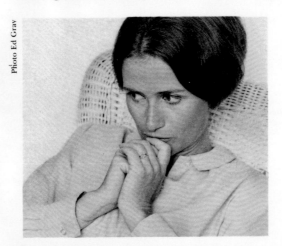

Nancy Wood lives in Colorado Springs—"across the Rockies" from her long-time friend Roy Stryker. When fourteen, she presented herself as "rather older" and acquired a job on a small newspaper in New Jersey. To date she has published numerous articles in major magazines, several novels, a volume of Indian poetry, and the Sierra Club book *Clearcut: The Deforestation of America*.

IN THIS PROUD LAND

AMERICA 1935-1943 AS SEEN IN THE F S A PHOTOGRAPHS

Roy Emerson Stryker and Nancy Wood

NEW YORK GRAPHIC SOCIETY LTD.
GREENWICH, CONNECTICUT

International Standard Book Number   0–8212–0521–8
Library of Congress Catalog Card Number   73–78792

First published 1973 by the New York Graphic Society Ltd.
140 Greenwich Avenue, Greenwich, Conn. 06830
First printing 1973

Printed by Rapoport Printing Corp., New York City
Designed by James Craig

Manufactured in U.S.A.

Contents

I. At home in Grand Junction, Colorado, Roy Stryker selecting FSA prints from his personal collection

George Croute

The FSA Collection of Photographs

by Roy Emerson Stryker

In 1935, Franklin D. Roosevelt established the Resettlement Administration as part of the New Deal. The basic responsibilities of RA included: Low-interest loans to poor farmers which would enable them to leave small or marginal tracts and become owners of productive land; land-renewal projects, such as reforestation; removal of certain families from cities where the economy would not sustain them to communal farms and well-ordered rural villages where they could become self-sufficient; and sponsorship of camps for migrant farm workers. The Department of Agriculture absorbed the RA early in 1937, and the Bankhead-Jones Farm Tenancy Act gave it legal status and a new name—The Farm Security Administration. [Ed.]

For nearly eight years, from 1935 to 1943, it was my great privilege to direct a small group of photographers working out of a grubby little government office in Washington, D.C. These gifted men and women of the Historical Section of the Farm Security Administration produced 270,000 pictures during that time. It is called a great collection now, perhaps the greatest ever assembled in the history of America. But I am not interested in adjectives. I am only interested in pictures.

And what pictures they were. I had no idea what was going to happen. I expected competence. I did not expect to be shocked at what began to come across my desk. The first three men who went out—Carl Mydans, Walker Evans and Ben Shahn—began sending in some astounding stuff that first fall, about the same time that I saw the great work Dorothea Lange was doing in California and decided to hire her. Then Arthur Rothstein, who had set up the lab, started taking pictures. Every day was for me an education and a revelation. I could hardly wait to get to the mail in the morning.

I especially remember one of Walker's early pictures—one of a cemetery and a stone cross, with some streets and buildings and steel mills in the background. Months after we'd released that picture a woman came in and asked for a copy of it. We gave it to her and when I asked her what she wanted it for, she said, "I want to give it to my brother who's a steel executive. I want to write on it, '*Your* cemeteries, *your* streets, *your* buildings, *your* steel mills. But *our* souls, God damn you.'"

Pictures like these were pretty heady. It was important that they came in when they did, so early in our experience. They gave me the first evidence of what we could do. They made it clear that the FSA collection was going to be something very special.

Just how special, though, we could not appreciate at the time. Sure, we had a sense that we were in on the beginning of something. In 1936 photography, which theretofore had been mostly a matter of landscapes and snapshots and family portraits, was fast being discovered as a serious tool of communications, a new way for a thoughtful, creative person to make a statement. Flash bulbs and small cameras were being used for the first

time. The rotogravure was dying; the first big picture magazines, which would take its place, were already being roughed out. In a year or so, and with a suddenness matched only by the introduction of television twelve years later, picture-taking became a national industry. We would have been insensitive indeed not to have realized that we were an important part of a movement.

In a sense, by experimenting freely with new forms and techniques, our unit was doing for professional photography what the WPA Theater was doing for the stage. Still, we had no idea that we were doing anything of the importance that later historians have credited us with. We particularly underestimated the content of our work. We know now that we helped open up a brand-new territory of American life and manners as a legitimate subject for visual commentary. We did not know it then. Day to day, we were too busy taking routine pictures for other Farm Security units, feeding pictures to newspapers, providing illustrations for reports and exhibits. There was one exception, however—and I guess I may as well admit it now. During the whole eight years, I held onto a personal dream that inevitably got translated into black-and-white pictures: I wanted to do a pictorial encyclopedia of American agriculture. My footnotes to the photographers' instructions ("keep your eyes open for a rag doll and a corn tester") undoubtedly accounted for the great number of photographs that got into the collection which had nothing to do with official business.

In truth, I think the work we did can be appreciated only when the collection is considered as a whole. The total volume, and it's a staggering volume, has a richness and distinction that simply cannot be drawn from the individual pictures themselves. There's an unusual continuity to it all. Mostly, there's rural America in it. It's the farms and the little towns and the highways between.

But most important, there is in this collection an attitude toward people. To my knowledge there is no picture in there that in any way whatsoever represents an attempt by a photographer to ridicule his subject, to be cute with him, to violate his privacy, or to do something to make a cliché. However they might have differed in skill and insight, our photographers had one thing in common, and that was a deep respect for human beings. Russell Lee's picture of the gnarled hands of the old woman, for instance—Russell took that with every degree of commiseration and respect. He wanted to say, "These are the hands of labor," and he said it eloquently. So it is all the way through the file. There's honesty there, and compassion, and a natural regard for individual dignity. These are the things that, in my opinion, give the collection its special appeal.

I think, too, that our work assumes particular significance when seen against the backdrop of contemporary photography as exemplified by the big picture magazines. By now, the bloom is off. Our eyes are literally assaulted by pictures every day. We're surfeited with pictures. But the problem is not so much that the public is used to pictures but that pictures are being badly used. Our editors, I'm afraid, have come to believe that the photograph is an end in itself. They've forgotten that the photograph is only the subsidiary, the little brother, of the word. Too many times nowadays the picture is expected to tell the whole story, when in truth there's only one picture in a hundred thousand that can stand alone as a piece of communication. As a result, news reporting itself has come to have a hurried, superficial, unsatisfying quality. Too often, too, the pictures are planned in advance by an editor who never sees the subject and there's no chance for the photographer's spontaneity to come through. Most of all, though, our big picture magazines were guilty of the same thing that's infected our movies, our theater, and our literature. Everything now has to happen on stage. Everything has to be shown, even the syphilis scabs.

I remember once at *Life* arguing with one of their photographers and a layout man. We were looking at a photograph of a man and a woman and a little girl. Their backs were to us. The woman was distraught. Her husband had his arm around her. The little girl at their side was winding up her overalls with one finger. The tension was unmistakable—the daughter of this man and woman had drowned in a lake and they were dragging for her. The little girl with them was their daughter's playmate. The *Life* men insisted that it would have been a better picture had the photographer taken it from the front. I could not possibly agree. Theirs was the attitude of the news photographer—always show the face, even if it's awkward—and I'm afraid that in too many instances the news photographer has taken over. This is to be regretted, I think, because too often what is communicated by this kind of overstatement, this reliance on the obvious, is not the essence of a situation but only the insincerity of the photographer.

In the light of what's happened since, it's clear that what we did at FSA constitutes a unique episode in the history of photography. And yet what was it precisely that we did? What, in a word, was our contribution?

Was it, for instance, art? Certainly we had some artists working for us. Walker Evans thought of his work as art and, to prove it, had a one-man show at the Museum of Modern Art. Ben Shahn, indubitably one of America's great moderns, was on the team; indeed, some of the scenes he took for us found their counterparts later in some of his oils. I remember sending young Jack Delano on assignment to Vermont. He spent hours asking himself, a bit self-consciously, "What is the *one* picture I can take that will say Vermont?" There's no question that photographers like these produced some great pictures, pictures that will live the way great paintings live. But is it art? Is any photography art? I've always avoided this particular controversy. Nothing strikes me as more

futile, and most of us in the unit felt the same way.

Was it sociology? I'm sure it was more than a little bit sociology. Ansel Adams, in fact, once told me, "What you've got are not photographers. They're a bunch of sociologists with cameras." When the author of *Middletown*, Bob Lynd, saw some of our pictures he got terribly excited and said, "This is a wonderful device for sociologists." He then got off onto a long discourse on the need to make people really *see*. "I wonder," he said, "how many people know what's even down their own street." Interestingly enough, one of the last boys I hired, John Collier, later developed a technique for using photographs to make people see more clearly "what's down their own street." He found that pictures frequently would stimulate seemingly inarticulate people into volunteering important anthropological data.

Was it journalism? Yes and no. We took news pictures, of course. We were in the same seedbed with *Life* and *Look,* for which some of our old staff later worked. (We are, as a matter of fact, said to have contributed substantially to the rise of photo-journalism. It would make just as much sense to speak of word-journalism. It seems to me that there's only journalism, plain and unhyphenated, and journalism consists of both words and pictures and sometimes you use more words than pictures and sometimes vice versa.) But we had no news photographers, as such. By this I mean we had no people especially gifted at knowing how to get to the dog fight, how to get to the place where the excitement was, point a camera, and get out. I think it's significant that in our entire collection we have only one picture of Franklin Roosevelt, the most newsworthy man of the era—this, mind you, in a collection that's sometimes said to have reported the feel and smell and taste of the thirties even more vividly than the news media. No, I think the best way to put it is that newspictures are the noun and the verb; our kind of photography is the adjective and adverb. The newspicture is a single frame; ours, a subject viewed in series. The newspicture is dramatic, all subject and action. Ours shows what's back of the action. It is a broader statement—frequently a mood, an accent, but more frequently a sketch and not infrequently a story.

Was it history? Of course. At least it was a slice of history. We provided some of the important material out of which histories of the period are being written. But you'll find no record of big people or big events in the collection. There are pictures that say labor and pictures that say capital and pictures that say Depression. But there are no pictures of sit-down strikes, no apple salesmen on street corners, not a single shot of Wall Street, and absolutely no celebrities.

Was it education? Very much so, and in more ways than one. For me, it was the equivalent of two Ph.D.'s and a couple of other degrees thrown in. I know it was an education to every photographer we had, too. And I'm sure it's made a contribution to public education.

If I had to sum it up, I'd say, yes, it was more education than anything else. We succeeded in doing exactly what Rex Tugwell said we should do: *We introduced Americans to America.* We developed the camera team, in contrast to the cameraman, and the full effect of this team's work was that it helped connect one generation's image of itself with the reality of its own time in history.

The reason we could do this, I think (and perhaps the reason it could never be done again), was that all of us in the unit were so personally involved in the times, and the times were so peculiarly what they were. It was a trying time, a disturbed time. None of us had suffered personally from the Depression, but all of us were living close to it, and when the photographers went out they saw a great deal of it. Curiously, though, the times did not depress us. On the contrary, there was an exhilaration in Washington, a feeling that things were being mended, that great wrongs were being corrected, that there were no problems so big they wouldn't yield to the application of good sense and hard work. There was apprehension, sure—but no apprehension to compare with our current fear of the bomb. There was a unifying source of inspiration, a great intelligence at work. It was called the New Deal and we were proud to be in on it. And with it all there was the willingness to strike out and do new things. You could do them, too, without fearing that somebody would take your job away or that you might be hauled before some Congressional committee and be made to confess your sins. There was a spirit in Washington that wrapped up our whole group. Some of us later came into positions of real authority. Some of us have even acquired what passes for fame. But I dare say that not one of us has felt more purposeful, or had more fun, than when at FSA.

I cannot, however, attribute the success of our unit entirely to the times. I can't dismiss it all as a product of the spirit of the thirties. I was in charge of the unit. I was given more freedom in the running of it than I had any reasonable right to expect, and whatever came of it, I was—as they say in government—both accountable and responsible. I never took a picture and yet I felt a part of every picture taken. I sat in my office in Washington and yet I went into every home in America. I was both the Stabilizer and the Exciter. Now at eighty I have the honesty to advance the somewhat immodest thought that it was my ideas, my biases, my passions, my convictions, my chemistry that held the team together and made of their work something more than a catalogue of celluloid rectangles in a government storehouse.

For thirty years I have waited to make my personal choice from the huge file that passed over my desk during those eight years. Partly it was because I did not wish to offend any photographer by leaning less toward his work than another's or by skipping over him entirely. I wanted no hard feelings among the fine people who worked for me. It has also been because the pictures needed to stew for a long time in my mind.

I have not chosen the greatest pictures from that file—although some of the greatest ones are included. I have chosen not on the basis of the artistic merit of a picture but on the basis of what each one represents to me in terms of intent. It is a purely personal choice and future historians may argue with me. Yet this selection states what one man—Roy Stryker—believed this country to be during a certain period of its history. On that assumption I have made what I hope is a valid and meaningful selection.

II. and III. Rothstein. *Couple who are FSA clients, Kersey, Colorado, 1939*
IV. Lee. *Woman at Sabine Farms, an FSA project; near Marshall, Texas, 1939*

Portrait of Stryker

by Nancy Wood

The Early Years

Roy Emerson Stryker was born in Great Bend, Kansas, in 1893, the son of George Stryker, a Civil War veteran, a radical Populist, and a man who was as much at home with the soil as he was with Socrates. Before long, the older Stryker moved his family to a ranch near Montrose, Colorado; here during the last days of the frontier, Roy Stryker grew up in raw and primitive surroundings. Yet at the center, at home, there were always books and family discussions about the latest political and economic theories. This foundation of earthiness and economics would help to establish him as one of the most important figures in the photographic world: the man who directed the taking of 270,000 pictures for the Farm Security Administration during the thirties.

Any review of Stryker's career reveals an unorthodox approach to whatever he undertook. His free style and self-reliance trace back to his early experiences in the West, where he punched cattle for seven years on his own homestead and worked in the nearby gold mines to supplement his income. They also can be attributed to the examples of people around him, particularly his father, whom he recalls as an extremist. "Dad was always trying new things and he tried them ten times harder than anybody else. If he went to take a patent medicine and the label said take one teaspoon, dad would down two tablespoons. If he read that a pinch of salt was good in coffee, he was just as likely to throw in a handful. And we all had to drink it, too. The same thing happened when he got religion from a circuit-riding preacher. We all had to get down on our knees in the evening and pray good and loud but nobody prayed louder than he did—especially at the end of one day when he had been out stumping for Populism. He started out all right, but all at once his political convictions got hold of him and at the top of his voice he prayed, 'Damn Wall Street, damn the railroads, and goddamn Standard Oil.'

"I often wonder what the old man would say if he knew I spent ten years of my life not only working for Standard Oil, but having a wonderful time at it."

During the First World War a slightly bewildered Stryker found himself in the homogenized ranks of the infantry. Yet there remained a considerable distinction between him and his fellow foot soldiers: his astounding—if not original—set of expletives, a distinction which has marked him all his days. Once, when a bureaucrat threatened his FSA project with extinction, Stryker described him as "a revolving son-of-a-bitch."

Returning home after the war, Stryker balked at going back to the Colorado School of Mines, where he had already put in two years studying to be a metallurgist. His brief glimpse of the East having furthered his basic drive and curiosity, he was ready for more challenging things. With a new bride at his side, Stryker headed for New York and enrolled at Columbia University.

"No greener kid ever hit Manhattan," he recalls. Registering at the majestic old Murray Hill Hotel, he spied a boy making off with his luggage and went after him, with invectives flying. The thief he cussed and caught was the bellhop.

During his first year in New York, Stryker ran out of money. Using his last nickel, he rode the subway downtown to one of Manhattan's most elegant hotels, where he paid a call on ex-governor William Sweet of Colorado. The two had never met before. Yet by the time he left, Stryker had secured a loan to tide him over the next few months. He paid it back regularly in small amounts and when the day came that his debt was settled, he was astonished to find that Sweet had given back $5.00 with the proviso that it not be used for any necessity. In his shabby clothes, with a few pennies in his pocket, Stryker took his wife to the opera.

New York led Stryker to a deepening social awareness. He lived in a tenement, and at first hand saw the plight of those with neither hope nor dignity. The faces of the downtrodden were on permanent exhibition in his mind; the small pleasures of the poor impressed him with the positive side of the human spirit. Provoked by the needs of others, and by his own need for a definite course of action, he plunged into the study of economics.

Eventually he began to thrive on the horizons that were opening to him. A lasting, though sometimes trying friendship was formed between Stryker and his economics professor, Rexford Guy Tugwell, later to become one of Roosevelt's brain-trusters and Stryker's mentor and employer in the Resettlement Administration, which evolved into the Farm Security Administration. The nature of their relationship is indicated by Stryker's humorous account of his first assignment from Professor Tugwell. "He was giving courses in Utopian Socialism and various other things. I had to write a paper and he said to me, 'If I don't like it, you'll get a D and if it isn't on time you'll get a D.'

"So I was late. And I got my paper back and the note on it said 'You're late but I'm giving you an A minus because it's typed and that's progress!'"

Tugwell's courses in economics set Stryker's mind afire. At the same time, Stryker became increasingly conscious of the power of photography—here was a prime means for documenting and publishing the conditions of the New York slums which had so aroused him. He studied the work of Lewis Hine and Jacob Riis, "absorbing social awareness through the pores."

Stryker completed his bachelor's degree and was nearly finished with his master's degree when, in 1924, he was appointed assistant in Columbia's Department of Economics. His approach to what was supposed to be a discussion of some problem raised by the professor's lecture set the administration's teeth on edge. This was the start of Stryker's role as a radical, not only in the teaching of economics but in documentary photography, where he was to make history. Stryker rebuffed the classic approach to teaching by declining to use a textbook. "What the hell," he growled some years later, "you can't learn about labor problems from print. You have to become involved in the dynamics of the thing by actually being there. And that's what we did. We went to labor meetings. We went to printing plants, banks, produce markets, slaughter houses, museums, and slums. I wanted the kids to see things for themselves.

"And that's where the use of pictures really began. I got impatient because the bright boys at Columbia had never seen a rag doll, a corn tester, or an old dasher churn. I dug up pictures to show city boys things that every farm boy knows about.

"Everywhere I went, I kept a pocket full of notes about my ideas for pictures. I wanted there to be a file on the things we were seeing but of course there wasn't.

"It was because of my interest in pictures that I lost my chance at a Ph.D. I thought I was a failure. I spent hours trying to figure out where I was going, what was going to become of me.

"But if I didn't know where I was going, my boss, Rex Tugwell, *did* know. He knew more about it than I did. He said to me, 'Roy, you'll never make an economist. But you can teach in another way—a better way—the way you know, with pictures.'

"He gave me the chance to do the illustrations for a book, *American Economic Life*—he also gave me the chance to be a co-author. Economists said it was sociology, sociologists said it was just a collection of pictures. But regardless of whether it was economics or sociology, it was a milestone in my relation to the photograph."

The process of gathering pictures for Tugwell's book was Stryker's first practical education in the use of photographs. He worked hard at the task of combing the files of the photo agencies but in the end it was Lewis Hine who supplied most of what he needed. Perhaps no other person had so much influence on Stryker as this aging documentary photographer, who would arrive at Columbia with armloads of pictures taken twenty years earlier. Ten years later the direction in which Stryker would aim his photographers was often reminiscent of the Hine approach. Even so, the small FSA team photographed with a head-on simplicity that was entirely their own.

For nearly ten years Stryker continued to teach at Columbia, continued his revolutionary field trips, continued to collect pictures for books which never materialized. Then came his break. Tugwell, one of Roosevelt's closest advisers and speech writers, was named Assistant Secretary of Agriculture and began to surround himself with college-trained intellectuals. Among them was Roy Stryker, his old student assistant.

The Depression Years

Stryker describes almost casually his transfer from the university campus to the national capital: "Tugwell went to Washington in the exciting early days of the New Deal and shortly thereafter he sent for me to come down and work with him. In this way he gave me my great chance. He wanted to prepare a pictorial documentation of our rural areas and rural problems, something that had always been dear to my heart.

"But I didn't know how to go about doing the job he wanted me to do—and he sensed it. One day he brought me into the office and said to me, 'Roy, a man may have holes in his shoes, and you may see the holes when you take the picture. But maybe your sense of the human being will teach you there's a lot more to that man than the holes in his shoes, and you ought to try and get that idea across.' "

That was in the summer of 1935. How was Stryker to picture what was behind the man with the holes in his shoes? He looked at his job description. His duties were to: "direct the activities of investigators, photographers, economists, sociologists and statisticians engaged in the accumulation and compilations of reports . . . , statistics, photographic material, vital statistics, agricultural surveys, maps and sketches necessary to make accurate descriptions of the various . . . phases of the Resettlement Administration, particularly with regard to the historical, sociological and economic aspects of the several programs and their accomplishments."

It was just the sort of vague governmental mumble that Stryker detested. Probably few men at the time were more ill-suited to government work than he and yet there he was, handed an unprecedented opportunity by Tugwell to do a particular job and to do it as he pleased. He knew there *had* to be a picture file of rural problems, but what kind of file and who would produce it?

Certainly not Stryker himself. Looking back at this time, he once remarked, "Perhaps my greatest asset was my lack of photographic knowledge. I didn't subscribe to anybody's particular school of photographic thought. I had what was then a strange notion—that pictures are pictures regardless of how they are taken. I was never a photographer. I was a teacher and gadgeteer, I always had a camera but I had no more business with that damn Leica than with a B-29. I got a hell of an inferiority complex because of it. My aunt and I once shot a family reunion. Her ten-dollar Brownie got everything while I drew blanks. I never snapped a shutter after that."

When Stryker arrived in Washington, photography in government was neither new nor uncommon. Mathew Brady's Civil War negatives had been filed away in the Signal Corps archives for seventy-five years. The Bureau of Reclamation had photographic records of the early

V. Rothstein. *Bootblack; corner of 14th Street and Eighth Avenue, New York City, 1937*

VI. Delano. *Watching removal of his grandson's household effects from the Pine Camp military area, near Watertown, New York, 1941*

Far West, a collection of 18 x 24 plate-glass negatives taken by William Henry Jackson. The Forest Service had pictures of the cut-and-get-out boom days in the timberlands. The Extension Service had a picture file on agriculture before the First World War. The fact is that there were many pictures—pictures filed away, indexed, and forgotten. And most of them routine. No life to them. No spark. Except for Brady's work, they portrayed nothing that would really move people.

"I'm the guy who sat in the middle," says Stryker."I kept the store. My title in Washington was Chief of the Historical Section. My goal was to write the history of the Farm Security Administration. We didn't collect many documents. We collected pictures. Many think I went down to Washington with a big plan. I didn't. There was no such plan."

There may not have been a plan, but there was a clear mandate from Tugwell. Get moving.

Slowly Stryker assembled his staff. The first to come was Arthur Rothstein, a chemistry major at Columbia who had taken a course in contemporary civilization under Stryker. At Columbia, Rothstein had also copied thousands of pictures for him for a book about agriculture. He was dependable, and a meticulous, skilled technician. He had just begun his photographic career by taking scientific pictures at a New York hospital. He would provide Stryker with the essentials of a darkroom.

Carl Mydans, with a strong background in journalism, was exploring everyday concerns with a camera in New York. Rejected by the magazines, which considered his 35mm Leica a toy, he was hired by Stryker, who cared nothing about his camera. He was impressed with Mydans' warm and spontaneous approach.

At the same time arrived the most prestigious, particular, and temperamental photographer on the FSA team—Walker Evans. His pictures stood out from the lot with a cold, stark, and unforgettable beauty. The only photographer to work with an 8 x 10 view camera, Evans took fewer pictures than anyone and spaced them over a longer period of time. Stryker eventually let him go because of his moodiness and his failure to produce the required number of photographs; the question of art was never involved. Today Evans' FSA pictures are regarded as the most artistic of all.

Soon after came Ben Shahn, a noted painter, lithographer, and muralist. Stryker recalls:

"Shahn came in from painting murals and I put a Leica in his hands and said, 'Go out and fool around with it.' Shahn came back with pictures that were like his paintings—imaginative, beautiful things not restricted by technique. They were often out of focus and overexposed or underexposed. When Arthur or Walker Evans or Carl Mydans would get to worrying too much about technique I'd bring out Shahn's photographs and say, 'Look at what Shahn has done and he doesn't know one part of a camera from another.' I wanted them to know how small a part the mechanical tool—the camera—played in making a good picture."

During that first year, Stryker saw the pictures of Dorothea Lange, who had been deeply involved with the plight of migrants in California. He was struck by her stark, merciless approach, yet her pictures reflected a dignity of spirit that was unique. Later Stryker said that Lange "had the most sensitivity and the most rapport with people." She was quickly added to the payroll.

The time was the fall of 1935. The FSA photo project moved into gear with five of the most gifted artists ever assembled. Although it was Stryker who guided and shaped the project for the next seven years, the photographers gave to Stryker a vision and an edge to his imagination that he had lacked before.

"I learned as much from the photographers as they did from me," he has readily admitted. "I respected them and counted on them and gave them hell.

"All we had was a rapport, a common desire to get the job done the best way we knew how. Above all, we were committed to honesty. Complete honesty is a very expensive affair. It is given to a few human beings to carry to its ultimate. I was one-half editor, one-half papa, one-half hell-raiser, one-half purchasing agent, and occasionally psychoanalyst without portfolio.

"And understand this. I was a man getting an education. I was having more vicarious pleasure from photography than anyone. I didn't have time to take pictures. I didn't need to."

The direction that the project took ignored governmental guidelines. Instead, Stryker's convictions went to work. "I have nothing of the craftsman about me at all," he once explained to a colleague. "My only implement in life has been an insatiable curiosity about everything and everybody."

Roy Stryker's desire for "what and why" showed up in his own, specific guidelines for the photographers. This was when Stryker—the teacher, the economist, the man capable of communicating his enthusiasm to his staff—was at his best.

Before going out on assignment, each member of the team was required to learn all he could about the area, its people, its economy, its political and social mores. The bible for the FSA photographers was J. Russell Smith's socio-economic geography book, *North America.* In addition they carried maps, USDA pamphlets, such magazines as *Harper's* and the *Atlantic,* plus a "shooting script" by Stryker which he has described as follows:

"Government was looser and more informal in those days than it is now. The bureaucratic web was such that my so-called official assignment memos—the photographers' shooting scripts—went like this: Bill posters; sign painters—crowd watching a window sign being painted; sky writing; paper in park after concert; parade

watching, ticker tape, sitting on curb; roller skating; spooners-neckers; mowing the front lawn."

Both Stryker's ability to direct and his insistence that photographers go out armed with the facts are amply illustrated by a story he tells about Carl Mydans:

"I remember one time when things were pretty bad down in the South and I assigned Carl to do a story about cotton. He had his bags packed and was going out the door and I said to him, 'I assume you know something about cotton.' He said, 'No, not very much.' I called in my secretary and said, 'Cancel Carl's reservations. He's going to stay here with me for a while.' We sat down and we talked almost all day about cotton. We went to lunch and we went to dinner and we talked well into the night about cotton. I told him about cotton as an agricultural product, cotton as a commercial product, the history of cotton in the South, what cotton did to the history of the country, and how it affected areas outside the country. By the time we were through, Carl was ready to go off and photograph cotton."

Two of the besetting sins of any bureaucracy are windy orders from above about how procedure should be carried out and foggy excuses from below about why orders have *not* been carried out. Stryker disdained both of them. He refused to use, or to be intimidated by, official jargon; and he would not tolerate any excuse for missing a picture. As he studied a shot, he would shout at the photographer, "Why did you take this picture? I don't care about the damn aesthetics—is it a good picture or not?"

His search was always for facts—meaning would speak for itself. The staff could not manufacture truth—it would show up by itself. As the photographs trickled back to Washington from the photographers, who sometimes went out for as long as six months at a time, Stryker knew what he was getting. He was excited and so were the publications which routinely published the pictures—at no cost—and brought to the attention of America what was happening to the one-third of a nation which was "ill-fed, ill-clad, and ill-housed." As a propaganda tool for the New Dealers to push through their farm program, the FSA pictures proved a vital asset. But they proved another thing, too. That America was not completely downtrodden, nor was it hopeless.

Yet the government was not concerned with the finer and more human aspects of what Stryker was doing. Again and again he was criticized for not sticking to business, for wasting taxpayers' money, for bootlegging into a government file a lot of silly pictures of American life that had no use whatsoever. There was a Congressional investigation. There were threats to cut off Stryker's funds. His staff was reduced. Time and again the photo unit seemed on the verge of oblivion. Time and again it was Tugwell who came to the rescue.

"The Administration," Stryker admitted many years

later, "simply could not afford to hammer home anything except their message that federal money was desperately needed for major relief programs. Most of what the photographers had to do to stay on the payroll was routine stuff showing what a good job the agencies were doing out in the field. That was my one compromise. Otherwise we would have been finished. But we got around all that bureaucratic red tape by throwing in a day here, a day there, to get what history has proved to be the guts of the project.

"I guess I would have to say that I had a pretty good hunch that the pictures that were ignored then were what would prove most valuable in the end. You can't have perspective when history is your bedfellow. All you have is a hunch. So I'd tell the photographers, look for the significant detail. The kinds of things that a scholar a hundred years from now is going to wonder about.

"They caught the significant detail all right. But sometimes it came a little too close for comfort. Like the summer of '36 when Arthur was out in the Dakotas and stumbled across the skull and horns of a steer bleaching in the sun. He reacted to the symbol of that skull in the midst of that dust-bowl country and he took a picture of it.

"That damn skull picture of Arthur's aroused more of an uproar than any other picture in history. It was an election year and they were looking for something to nail Roosevelt with. Some editor out there in Dakota spotted the fact that Arthur had used different backgrounds and right away he labeled it a phony. Pretty soon front pages all over the country were saying the FSA was using phony pictures. The government publicists began to squirm. There was going to be an investigation. I called Arthur in and said, 'What about this damn skull?' And he said that all he'd done was to move it about ten feet to get a slightly better background for the second shot. So I said to the government boys, 'What the hell. The point of the picture is that there's a drought. Cattle are dying. And don't tell me that the photographer got out of the drought area by moving ten feet.' I don't think anyone questioned the FSA pictures after that."

What exactly was Stryker after? As his staff shifted so did his ideas. What had started out as a picture file for propaganda purposes became the most powerful photographic statement of all time. By then, new people were working under the Stryker aegis: Russell Lee, Marion Post, John Collier, Jr., John Vachon, Jack Delano and, toward the end, Gordon Parks, the gifted black photographer.

Stryker developed a unique relationship with Russell Lee which has lasted to the present day. "One photographer stood out from all the others and that was Russell. Not because he was better than the others, but because there was some quality in Russell that helped me through

my problems. It was the kind of relationship between two guys that have been through the war together. When his photographs would come in, I always felt that Russell was saying, 'Now here is a fellow who is having a hard time but with a little help he's going to be all right.' And that's what gave me courage."

From 1937 until the demise of the project in 1943, Stryker and his people were constantly seeking broader dimensions. It was Stryker's goal to "record on film as much of America as we could in terms of people and the land. We photographed destitute migrants and average American townspeople, sharecroppers and prosperous farmers, eroded land and fertile land, human misery and human elation. Many of these people were sick, hungry, and miserable. The odds were against them. Yet their goodness and strength survived.

"What we ended up with was as well-rounded a picture of American life during that period as anyone could get. The pictures that were used were mostly pictures of the dust bowl and migrants and half-starved cattle. But probably half of the file contained positive pictures, the kind that give the heart a tug.

"But the faces to me were the most significant part of the file. When a man is down and they have taken from him his job and his land and his home—everything he spent his life working for—he's going to have the expression of tragedy permanently on his face. But I have always believed that the American people have the ability to endure. And that is in those faces, too. Remember Steinbeck's famous lines—'We ain't gonna die out. People is goin' on'? That's the feeling which comes through in those pictures. Every single one. Experts have said to me, oh no, that's a face of despair. And I say, look again, you see the set of that chin. You see the way that mother stands. You see the straight line of that man's shoulders. You see something in those faces that transcends misery.

"I remember when Steinbeck came in and looked at the pictures for a couple of days. Those tragic, beautiful faces were what inspired him to write *The Grapes of Wrath*. He caught in words everything the photographers were trying to say in pictures. Dignity versus despair. Maybe I'm a fool, but I believe that dignity wins out. When it doesn't, then we as a people will become extinct."

The shift in Stryker's direction had far-reaching results. For not only did the Historical Section of the FSA move decisively out from its original role as a propaganda agency but the new, broad, and positive view of America was hungrily grabbed up by news agencies and magazines throughout the country. The cross index revealed a fascinating profile of America. Covered were: courthouses, town halls, gas stations, barber shops, privies; among activities listed were strikes, auctions, side shows, drinking, gambling, parades, loafing. Groups of people included Negroes, Mexicans, Indians, Cajuns, mountaineers. Some eighteen crops were covered, from cotton to cranberries. Under "Culture of the U.S." were listed the American roadside, interiors, primitive paintings, movies, religion, radio, signs, and on and on.

Stryker's shooting scripts often went far beyond simple instructions. They assigned subjects, raised questions, and contained comments that no cameramen had ever encountered before. In one script, Stryker requested pictures showing "that the American highway is very often a more attractive place than the places Americans live." In another, he asked for a shot from Kansas suggesting "that there is nothing in the world that matters very much but wheat." His small-town script asked questions like "What keeps the town going?," and "How do people spend their evenings—show this at varied income levels." It also requested scenes like back porches, the details of which "may be quite revealing," and one showing "the edge of town—where the town and country meet (a difficult thing to show)."

The town pictures had a curious effect on Stryker, taking him back to the scene of his youth in Montrose, Colorado. In his own words: "Through the pictures the small town emerged as a thing possessing emotional and esthetic advantages: kinship with nature and the seasons, neighborliness, kindliness, spaciousness—plus some certain disadvantages: laziness, pompousness, narrowness, lack of economic and cultural freedom.

"I remember Walker Evans' picture of the train tracks in a small town, like Montrose. The empty station platform, the station thermometer, the idle baggage carts, the quiet stores, the people talking together, and beyond them, the weatherbeaten houses where they lived, all this reminded me of the town where I had grown up. I would look at pictures like that and long for a time when the world was safer and more peaceful. I'd think back to the days before radio and television when all there was to do was go down to the tracks and watch the flyer go through. That was the nostalgic way in which those town pictures hit me.

"Arthur once took a shot of a wonderful old Maine couple who lived in a town. On it Archibald MacLeish wrote, 'The real test of democracy may come in the towns.' History proved him right. During the war, the rural people were called upon to feed our armed forces. They were important. They had a job to do and they rose to the occasion. The growing, the shipping, the booming of their little businesses—this was democracy all right. Afterwards, they were not so important anymore. A lot of people died and a lot of people moved away. There settled over those little towns a permanent wistfulness."

Stryker's focus on America's small towns eventually produced a realization within the government that the economic and social deprivations of the rural community had their counterparts in the city. Although Stryker was

VII. Lee. *A radiator cap; Laurel, Mississippi, 1939*

VIII. Lee. *New Iberia, Louisiana, 1938*

no longer harassed for his "silly sentimental pictures of women in bonnets," further pressure was put on him to deliver mundane illustrations for the Department of Agriculture and the Department of Public Health.

Still, after three years of existence, the work of the FSA group was zeroing in on fundamental aspects of rural life. A whole new outlook and sophistication gripped the photographers who had worked so long with rural people. They began to function as reporters, feeding back to Stryker graphic descriptions of why and where unrest and injustice were building up. And he, in turn, would see that the information worked its way into the right channels for government action. He once remarked, "This was all part of our job to record contemporary history. That's why I was once startled—though not displeased—when someone called me 'a press agent of the underprivileged.' "

Wartime

Press agent though he might have been, Stryker was also a watchdog of the national image. One day shortly before the Germans launched their attack in Europe, a well-dressed gentleman from the German embassy showed up at Stryker's office, asking to be shown the "famous" pictures of America—the sharecroppers and migrants, floods and dust storms, and other scenes of woe and misery that had been printed across America. Said Stryker: "He was a very pleasant little Nazi. I had no intention of allowing the records of America's internal problems to fall into his hands. I had the file clerks show him a wonderful range of things—mountains and rivers and lush fields, well-dressed people living off what fat there was left of the land. He left without having chosen a single one."

As clouds of war began to loom on the horizon, Stryker sent his team to find out what effects the build-up for war was having on the people and the land. Yet assignments to cover an aircraft works would also contain classic Stryker instructions to cover the rural scene. Jack Delano's first trip to photograph the rural northeast in the fall of 1940 was begun with a note to "Please watch for autumn pictures, as calls are beginning to come in for them and we are short. These should be rather the symbol of Autumn . . . cornfields, pumpkins. . . . Emphasize the idea of abundance—the 'horn of plenty'—and pour maple syrup over it—you know, mix well with white clouds and put on a sky-blue platter. I know your damned photographer's soul writhes, but to hell with it. Do you think I give a damn about a photographer's soul with Hitler at our doorstep? You are nothing but camera fodder to me."

Replied Delano, after obediently photographing a commercial poultry farm: "Who the hell can get excited about a chicken?"

Another memo to Delano, who was about to make a foray into Georgia, revealed a more serious intent on the part of his chief. Delano was to get:

"Soldiers on the street corners, soldiers playing pinball machines, soldiers playing those little machine guns (target practice).

"I am very anxious that we get additional pictures of the soldiers' life around the towns near big encampments. You can emphasize the congestion in the town and the blocking up of normal facilities caused by the soldiers coming into towns for the weekends. . . . You should by all means try your hand at Phoenix City. Most of the prostitution is on that side of the river. . . . Try to get . . . a soldier, lonely, trying to pick up a date."

Soldiers, civilians—all the human lives caught up in the war effort touched Stryker as deeply as the migrants and the sharecroppers had a decade earlier. He believed that the nation, toughened by the Depression, would have new purpose, new agressiveness—and new dimension. Excitedly, he began to plan to cover the home front in much the same way as he had the FSA programs. His team would dutifully record the shipyards, the victory gardens, and the boot camps, but it would also record the soul of a nation as well.

Up to December 7, 1941 the well-established Historical Section had pretty much carte blanche in covering the nation's build-up the way Stryker wanted it done. But after Pearl Harbor, bureaucratic changes, a cutback in funds, and a Congressional assault on the FSA wiped out all hopes that Stryker had for a meaningful study of America emerging as the major world power. For nearly two years he fought to keep his project alive, sending photographers into the field to gather some of the most poignant shots to come out of the section. But in September 1943, knowing that the nature of his job had changed, Stryker resigned. To the astonishment of many of his colleagues, he went to work for Standard Oil, building a legendary—and oft-imitated—collection of industrial pictures.

Speaking of his days at Farm Security, Stryker once remarked, "Had they known I was going to turn the place upside down, they probably would have fired me. My attitude was to hell with Capitol Hill. The pictures were the important thing. To spend all that money (nearly a million dollars) to get all those pictures (nearly 270,000) was something of a bureaucratic miracle. Toward the end, there was strong pressure from the government to destroy the entire file, negatives included. For a time it looked like everything would be lost. Then my old friend Archibald MacLeish appeared as head of the Library of Congress. I had always wanted the collection to go there and so it did, narrowed down to 170,000 negatives."

16

Of the 70,000 pictures on file at the Library of Congress, an estimated 40,000 are of agricultural programs, dedications and the war effort. The discrepancy between the 70,000 file pictures and the 170,000 negatives is accountable for the most part to duplication of subject material. Of the 270,000 photographs actually taken during the project's lifetime, Stryker killed—by punching holes in the negatives—about 100,000.

The FSA photo project was unique. Not only were the times and people right, but Roy Stryker was certainly right. Asked once whether there could ever again be such a project, Stryker replied, "It was all just a little like the process of evolution that I learned about years ago at the Colorado School of Mines. When the water temperature was right, when the salts in the river were right, the salamanders came out of the water and pretty soon human beings were created. Now, do you know what the water temperature down in Washington is? Do you know if the salts are right? Well, don't come out of the water until you do."

Then he added, "Farm Security was one of those freaks, one of those salamanders. It can't happen again. But something new will happen. Something different. I wish to hell I could be around to do it."

The Year of In This Proud Land

In his eightieth year, Roy Stryker was living in Grand Junction, Colorado, not far from the barren sage country where he had grown up. He had moved back west in 1962, the same year that an exhibition of FSA pictures, "The Bitter Years," opened at the Museum of Modern Art in New York. It was in the great galleries there that I first met him, standing amid the 171 large pictures which Edward Steichen had selected to represent what America was during the Depression. Stryker was then sixty-nine, with a shock of white hair . . . a wiry, witty man with a trip-hammer flow of speech. Although he was impressed with "The Bitter Years," he was disappointed that Steichen had not selected any of what he called "the positive pictures." "Steichen's approach," he said later, "was to show misery in its finest hour—not one damn bit of humor. The point was 'The Bitter Years' and that is what was shown."

We were drawn together almost instantly, he an enthusiastic teacher and critic who kept answering my questions about the pictures, and I a writer with a deep interest in photography. We saw each other from time to time, in Montrose and later in Grand Junction, spending hours going over his file of prints and contact sheets from the FSA project. I never tired of looking at them. From Stryker I learned a great deal. About pictures. About the Depression years—which I was born too late

to remember. And about the fabric of life itself.

Partly to offset the negativism of "The Bitter Years" and partly to dispel the widely held belief that the FSA pictures were *all* downbeat, Stryker felt he had to do a book. Besides, he had not made a definitive statement about the pictures or FSA. He decided it was time.

My job was to help him crystallize his thoughts, to share in the picture selection, to do the legwork and to write about Stryker himself—over his vehement objections. "Goddamn it," he would say, "why are you writing all this down? People are interested in the pictures, not Stryker." When we were looking at the pictures together he would often demand, "What have you learned? What do you see? Can you tell me why this is a good picture?" At eighty, he was still the teacher and the rugged taskmaster.

In the spring of 1972 Stryker began to select a representative group of pictures from his private collection for the book. Its theme he described as "lost America"—a phrase deliberately ambiguous. Looking at the pictures one day, Stryker said to me, "I know what's wrong with this country. They've lost the important things. They've hardened up. They don't give a damn anymore. You look at these pictures before people lost—what? The ability to care. The ability to take joy in simple pleasures. The ability to take life however it came.

"You could look at the people and see fear and sadness and desperation. But you saw something else, too. A determination that not even the Depression could kill. The photographers saw it—documented it.

"Sure, the kids looked grim sometimes. So did their parents. Nobody had a dime. But they had a whole lot more. They had each other, as corny as that sounds today. A family stuck together. It's all there was. They did such simple things. A man would sit on a street corner for hours, talking to his friends. What would they talk about? I don't know. It didn't matter so long as somebody listened. Who listens now?

"Take that farm woman out in Nebraska. Putting up peaches or tomatoes or beans. Bone tired, dead broke, old before her time. What was her reward? Something of herself in that row of Mason jars on the shelf. Her eyes would tell you that. And that little sharecropper's boy. What did he ever know except misery? But look at him close. A natural dignity in the way he stands.

"I ask myself, where has it all gone. Why don't people care about each other anymore?"

He would shake his head and look out the window toward the land he had known as a boy. He was disturbed about what had happened to the country. He complained about technology and the way it had displaced the old value system. He railed against the dehumanizing aspects of government. He was disgusted with the erosion of human rights. Clearly, he longed for life as he had once known it. And through the file of pictures that he always

IX. Lange. *Migrant mother; Nipomo, California, 1936*

kept with him, he could re-live it any time he wished.

Stryker had selected 1300 prints before he left Washington in 1943 to go to work for Standard Oil. They had been kept in his desk for thirty years and he would take them out now and then, "to see why I had selected those particular thirteen hundred. To ask myself what they stood for and would they hold up. If I went back to the Library of Congress now and went through that whole damn bunch, I might select a hundred more. But I don't think so. Because here is the essence."

It was this collection of 1300 prints, on contact sheets and in 5 x 7 print form, that Stryker and I worked on all through the spring and summer of 1972. The choice, always and finally, was his.

One by one he would lay out the pictures. Then he would circle around them, turning face down the ones he didn't want. Occasionally he would pick up a photograph and discuss it: perhaps a prairie landscape—"This is big country"; or a scene of children—"No shoes but, damn it, you just know they're nice kids"; or a picture of a Thanksgiving dinner—"We tried to mirror the American scene and nothing is as American as apple pie—though I suspect these pies are mince"; or a view of migrants— ". . . their hopes buried in the burned-out soil. They packed their belongings and moved on. A tragic piece of history. It needed to be recorded."

One day in September, as Stryker was moving around the tables, he came across Dorothea Lange's picture of the migrant mother, the most famous to come out of the FSA Collection. He stopped and looked at it a long time. The print was mounted, and much larger than the rest. He had gone into his bedroom to get it and I'd wondered why he kept it apart from the others.

I said nothing as I watched him sink deeper and deeper into thought. We had never spoken about this particular picture in all the years we had been friends. He had, in fact, kept it hidden from view. I knew very little about it except that it had been taken in 1936 by Lange in the pea fields of California. While Stryker sat with the picture, I dug through the file and found Lange's account of it. She had written:

"I saw and approached the hungry and desperate mother, as if drawn by a magnet. I do not remember how I explained my presence or my camera to her, but I do remember she asked me no questions. I made five exposures, working closer and closer from the same direction. I did not ask her name or her history. She told me her age, that she was 32. She said that they had been living on frozen vegetables from the surrounding fields, and birds that the children killed. She had just sold the tires from her car to buy food. There she sat in that lean-to tent with her children huddled around her, and she thought that my pictures might help her, and so she helped me."

Stryker finally turned to me and said: "When Dorothea took that picture, that was the ultimate. She never surpassed it. To me, it was *the* picture of Farm Security. The others were marvelous but that was special. Notice I never said it was the greatest. People would say to me, that migrant woman looks posed and I'd say she does *not* look posed. That picture is as uninvolved with the camera as any picture I've ever seen. They'd say, well, you're crazy and I'd say I'm not crazy. I'll stand on that picture as long as I live.

"After all these years, I still get that picture out and look at it. The quietness and the stillness of it. . . . Was that woman calm or not? I've never known. I cannot account for that woman. So many times I've asked myself what is she thinking? She has all of the suffering of mankind in her but all of the perseverance too. A restraint and a strange courage. You can see anything you want to in her. She is immortal. Look at that hand. Look at the child. Look at those fingers—those two heads of hair."

He was never again more eloquent—or revealing— about any of the Farm Security pictures.

During the preparation of this book, I went to the Library of Congress, where I examined the entire FSA Collection of prints—some 70,000 of them, beautifully filed, captioned, and mounted on cardboard. I had arrived in Washington with admiration for the depth of Stryker's vision; I came away in awe at its breadth. His vision indeed had produced a national treasure.

By the end of 1972, Stryker had ended up with about 200 pictures, less than one tenth of one percent of all that had been shot. They were, for him, the summing up of his own life as well as being one of the most powerful statements about America ever made. "My reputation," he said on the day we were finally finished, "may be there in the file in Washington. But here is where my credo is."

I have not chosen the greatest pictures . . .
although some of the greatest ones are included.
I have chosen not on the basis of the artistic merit
of a picture but on the basis of what each one
represents to me in terms of intent.

1. Rothstein. *Dalton, New York, 1937*

2. Lange. *Tulare County, California, 1938*

3. Post Wolcott. *Near Wadesboro, North Carolina, 1938*

4. (overleaf) Vachon. *Monona County, Iowa, 1940*

5. Lange. *Hoe culture; Alabama*

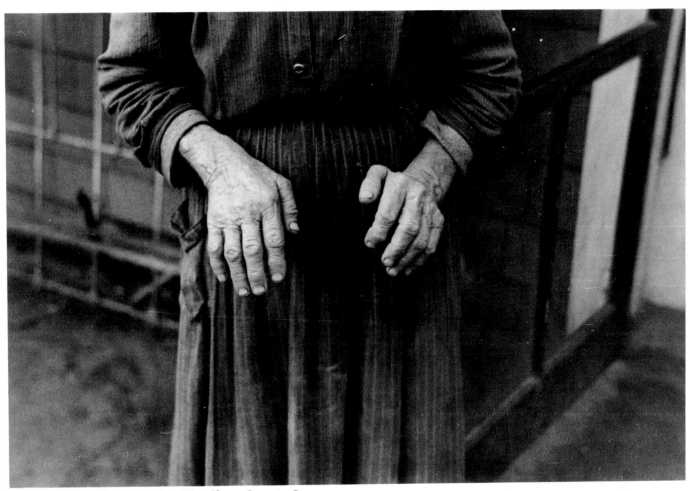

6. Lee. *Wife of a homesteader; Woodbury County, Iowa*

7. Lee. *San Marcos, Texas, 1940*

8. Shahn. *On duty during strike; Morgantown, West Virginia, 1935*

9. Lee. *Donaldsonville, Louisiana, 1938*

10. Lee. *Visiting a relative's grave on All Saints Day; New Roads, Louisiana, 1938*

11. Delano. *Greene County, Georgia, 1941*

12. Lee. *School children at FSA farm workers' camp; Caldwell, Idaho, 1941*

13. (right) Vachon. *Richland County, Wisconsin, 1942*

Not a single shot of Wall Street,
and absolutely no celebrities

14. Lee. *Mound Bayou, Louisiana, 1939*

15. Shahn. *A citizen who has lost his farm—and his sight and hearing; Circleville, Ohio, 1938*

16. Post Wolcott. *Changing a tire—with a fencepost as a jack; South Fork of the Kentucky River, Kentucky, 1940*

17. Lee. *New Madrid County, Missouri, 1938*

18. Lee. *Pie Town, New Mexico, 1940*

19. Post Wolcott. *One of the judges at the horse races; Warrenton, Virginia, 1941*

20. Lange. *Greene County, Georgia, 1937*

GREAT NORTHERN
34677

CAPACITY 80000
LOAD LIMIT 93600
TARE 42400 F.8 38
TOTAL Wt. 136000
CUBIC CAPY. 2089 ft.

SEE AMERICA FIRST
GLACIER NATIONAL PARK

40 FEET.

21. Vachon. *Minneapolis, Minnesota, 1939*

22. (right) Rothstein. *Waiting for the train; Hagerstown, Maryland, 1937*

23. Delano. *Polish family; Mauch Chunk, Pennsylvania, 1940*

24. Lee. *In front of the courthouse; San Augustine, Texas, 1939*

25. Delano. *Stonington, Connecticut, 1940*

26. Shahn. *Mountain fiddler; Asheville, North Carolina, 1937*

27. Lee. *Farmer's wife; Black River Falls, Wisconsin, 1937*

28. Bubley. *Memorial Day; Arlington Cemetery, Virginia, 1941*

29. Delano. *Union Point, Georgia, 1941*

30. Lee. *Wrestling match sponsored by American Legion; Sikeston, Missouri, 1938*

31. Lee. *Winton, Minnesota, 1937*

32. Lee. *An East Texan; Jacksonville, Texas, 1939*

33. Shahn. *Cattle dealer; West Virginia, 1935*

34. Shahn. *Strawberry pickers' child; Louisiana, 1935*

35. Lange. *80-year-old resident in squatters' camp; Bakersfield, California, 1936*

36. Lee. *A homesteader; Pie Town, New Mexico, 1940*

37. Rothstein. *Virginia, 1936*

38. Post Wolcott. *Rural Rehabilitation client; Greene County, Georgia, 1939*

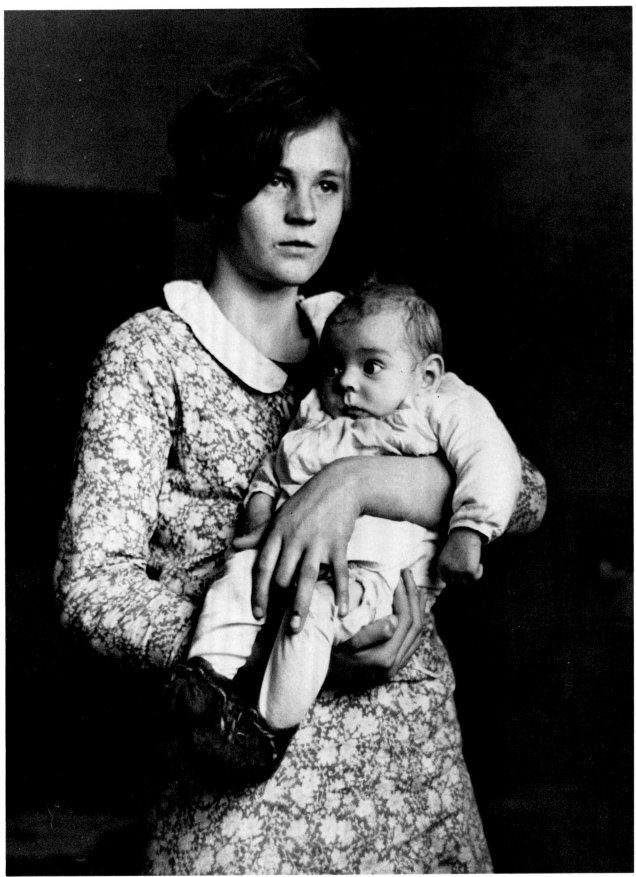

39. Lee.*Refugees in a schoolhouse; Sikeston, Missouri*

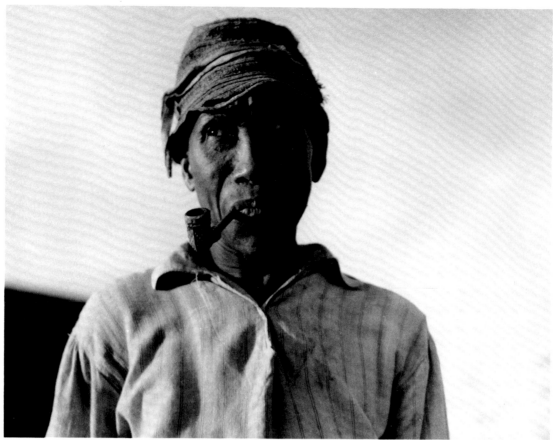

40. Lange. *Resident on plantation; near Leland, Mississippi, 1937*

41. Lange. *Resident at irrigation project; Malheur County, Oregon, 1939*

42. Rothstein. *Eden Mills, Vermont*

43. Evans. *Sharecropper's daughter; Hale County, Alabama, 1935*

44. Rothstein. *Blue Ridge Mountains, Virginia*

45. Collins. *Mennonite couple; Pennsylvania*

46. Lee. *Fortune teller at State Fair; Donaldsonville, Louisiana, 1938*

47. Vachon. *Meeker County, Minnesota, 1942*

There are pictures that say labor
and pictures that say capital
and pictures that say Depression.

48. Lange. *Plantation owner; near Clarksdale, Mississippi, 1936*

49. Collins. *Lancaster, Pennsylvania, 1942*

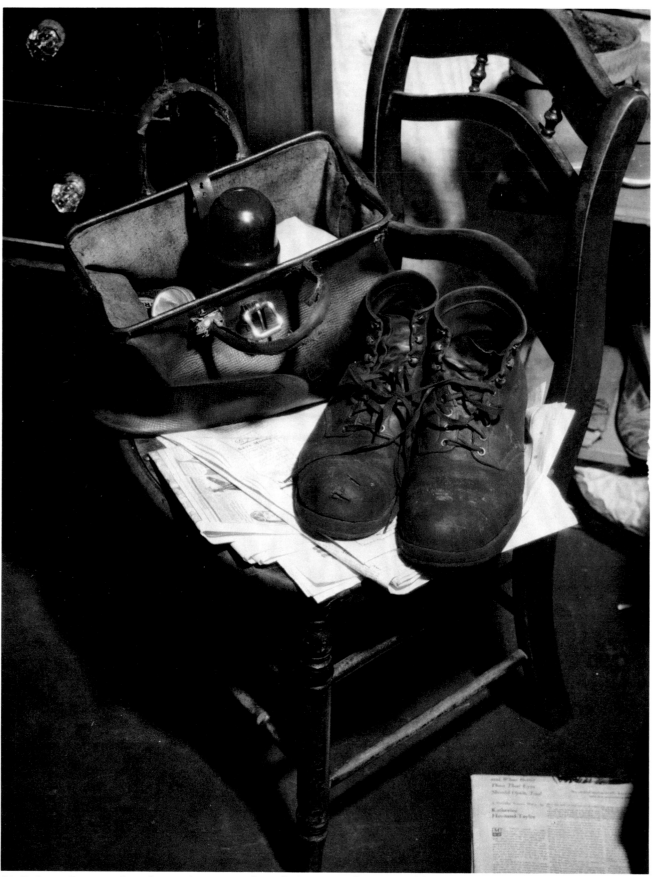

50. Delano. *Items to be taken to Boston steel works by a part-time vegetable farmer; Saugus, Massachusetts, 1941*

51. Evans. *Bethlehem, Pennsylvania*

52. Vachon. *Traveling salesman in hotel lobby; Elkins, West Virginia, 1939*

53. Delano. *A renter plowing sweet potatoes; Greene County; Georgia, 1941*

54. Delano. *Indiana Harbor Beltline Railroad yard, Indiana, 1943*

55. Lee. *Rancher at county fair; Gonzales, Texas, 1939*

56. Vachon. *Worker at carbon black plant; Sunray, Texas, 1942*

57. Lee. *Shasta Dam, California, 1941*

58. Mydans. *Migrants on the road—"Damned if we'll work for what they pay folks hereabouts"; Crittenden County, Arkansas, 1936*

59. Delano. *Coal miner; near Penfield, Pennsylvania*

60. Lange. *Spring plowing in cauliflower fields; Guadalupe, California, 1937*

61. Rothstein. *Proprietor of restaurant; Shellpile, New Jersey, 1938*

62. Lee. *Cattlemen at auction of prize beef steers and breeding stock; San Angelo, Texas, 1940*

63. Post Wolcott. *Coal miner's child taking home a can of kerosene; Pursglove, Scott's Run, West Virginia, 1938*

Nobody had a dime.
But they had a whole lot more.
They had each other.

64. Lee. *FSA clients at home; Hidalgo County, Texas, 1939*

65. Post Wolcott. *Son of recipient of an FSA loan; Knox County, Kentucky, 1940*

66. Rothstein. *Unemployed mine worker; Bush, Illinois, 1939*

67. Lee. *Lumberjack in saloon; Craigville, Minnesota, 1937*

68. Post Wolcott. *Farmer and children; Natchitoches, Louisiana, 1940*

69. Lee. *At an all-day community sing; Pie Town, New Mexico, 1940*

70. Post Wolcott. *Jitterbugging in a juke joint on Saturday night; Clarksdale, Mississippi, 1939*

71. Delano. *Farm children; Carroll County, Georgia, 1941*

72. Vachon. *Berkeley Springs, West Virginia, 1939*

73. Lee. *Cat nap after the Fourth of July parade; Vale, Oregon, 1941*

74. Rothstein. *Young married couple; Dyess County, Arkansas*

Those tragic, beautiful faces . . .

75. Vachon. *Ozark Mountains, Missouri, 1940*

76. Lee. *Migrant child returning home from fields; Prague, Oklahoma, 1939*

77. Lange. *Born a slave, resettled after the Civil War; Carrizo Springs, Texas, 1936*

78. Lange. *Drought refugee; Oklahoma, 1937*

79. Carter. *Family stricken by tuberculosis; Albany County, New York, 1936*

80. Lange. *Drought refugees from Oklahoma; Blythe, California, 1936*

81. Evans. *Cotton sharecropper; Hale County; Alabama, 1935*

82. Lange. *Refugee from southeast Missouri flood; Westley, California, 1939*

83. Rothstein. *Man and Model T Ford that makes 100 miles a day in flight from grasshopper- and drought-ridden area of South Dakota; Highway 10, Missoula, Montana, 1936*

84. (overleaf) Lee. *Box Elder County, Utah, 1940*

85. Lange. *Kern County, California, 1937*

86. Post Wolcott. *near Bardstown, Kentucky, 1940*

87. Lee. *Traveling evangelists, still preaching the gospel and sharpening knives to pay expenses after 25 years on the road; near Scott, Louisiana, 1938*

88. Vachon. *Riding the ranch in the rigors of winter; Lyman County, South Dakota*

89. Post Wolcott. *Shenandoah Valley, Virginia*

101. Rothstein. *Farm family; St. Charles County, Missouri, 1939*

102. Rothstein. *Oklahoma*

103. Rothstein. *Garrett County, Maryland, 1936*

104. Rothstein. *Dawes County, Nebraska, 1939*

105. Evans. *Country store; near Moundville, Alabama, 1935*

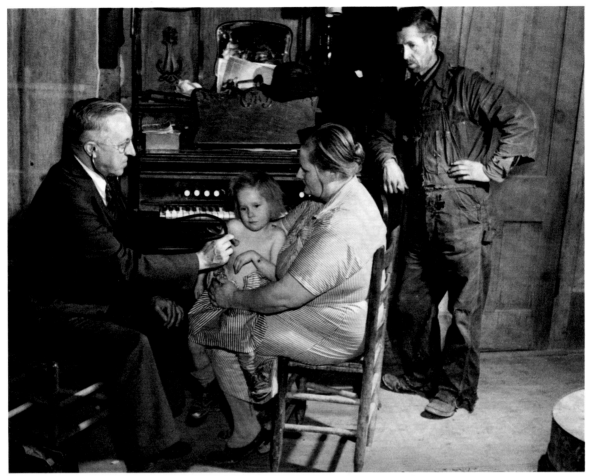

106. Vachon. *Country doctor and patient in farm home; Scott County, Missouri, 1942*

107. Post Wolcott. *Rural one-room schoolhouse; Breathitt County, Kentucky, 1940*

108. Delano. *A moment off from chopping cotton; Greene County, Georgia, 1941*

109. Delano. *On hand to help a neighbor plant tobacco; Durham, North Carolina, 1940*

110. Lee. *Orange County, Vermont, 1939*

111. Rothstein. *Cutting hay; Vermont*

112. **Delano.** *Barnside art; near Thompsonville, Connecticut, 1940*

113. Vachon. *Playing "Cut the Pie" and "Fox and Geese" during noon recess at rural school; Morton County, North Dakota, 1942*

114. Shahn. *Talking politics before dinner at wheat-harvest time; Central Ohio, 1938*

*The small town emerged as a thing
possessing emotional and esthetic advantages:
kinship with nature and the seasons,
neighborliness, kindliness, spaciousness—
plus some certain disadvantages.*

115. Evans. *Edwards, Mississippi*

116. Shahn. *Natchez, Mississippi*

117. Post Wolcott. *Woodstock, Vermont*

118. Shahn. *Linworth, Ohio*

119. Shahn. *Omar on Scott's Run, West Virginia, 1935*

120. Evans. *Beyond the entrance, tents for flood refugees, Marianna, Arkansas, 1937*

121. Lange. *Town suffering from the Depression and from the drought in surrounding farmland; Caddo, Oklahoma, 1938*

122. Evans. *Atlanta, Georgia, 1936*

123. Shahn. *Mechanicsburg, Ohio, 1938*

124. Lange. *Eden, Alabama, 1936*

125. Lange. *Migrant who follows the fruit; San Joaquin Valley, California, 1938*

126. Evans. *A boardinghouse; Birmingham, Alabama, 1936*

127. Lee. *Arlington, Vermont, 1938*

128. Evans. *Easton, Pennsylvania, 1935*

129. Lee. *Farmer waiting for garage man; near Amite, Louisiana, 1938*

130. Lee. *Roadside camp of migrant workers; Lincoln County, Oklahoma, 1939*

131. Evans. *Streetside games; New York City, 1938*

132. Vachon. *Lighted porch to welcome visitors; Pierre, South Dakota, 1940*

133. Post Wolcott. *Greene County, Georgia, 1939*

134. Vachon. *Memphis, Tennessee, 1940*

135. Rothstein. *Railroad avenue; Winslow, Arkansas, 1935*

136. Delano. *Gypsy child on U.S. 13; near Salisbury, Maryland, 1940*

*To my knowledge there is no picture that in any way
whatsoever represents an attempt by a photographer to ridicule
his subject, to be cute with him, to violate his privacy,
or to do something to make a cliché*

137. Lange. *Revival meeting in a garage; Dos Palos, California, 1938*

138. Shahn. *Sharecropper family; Mississippi*

139. Delano. *Prelude to afternoon meal; Carroll County, Georgia, 1941*

140. Lee. *Dressed up for the show; Chicago, Illinois, 1941*

141. Delano. *Sunday morning; White Plains, Georgia, 1941*

142. Collier. *The mayor—unable to speak English but fascinated by pictures of far-off places; Trampas, New Mexico, 1943*

143. Lee. *Instruction at home; Transylvania, Louisiana, 1939*

144. Lange. *San Francisco, California, 1939*

145. Post Wolcott. *Baptismal service; Morehead, Kentucky, 1940*

146. Rothstein. *Christmas window; Oswego County, New York, 1937*

146

147. Lee. *Day laborers' sons who have never attended school; Webbers Falls, Oklahoma, 1939*

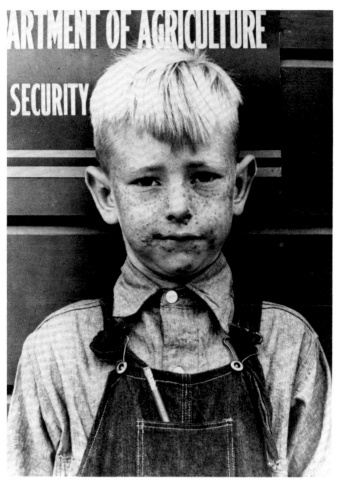

148. Rothstein. *Migrant child; Visalia, California, 1940*

149. Lee. *Corpus Christi, Texas, 1939*

150. Post Wolcott. *Coal miner's child using the cat hole; Bertha Hill on Scott's Run, West Virginia, 1938*

151. Lee. *Son of sharecropper; Southeast Missouri, 1938*

152. Lee. *Daughter of sharecropper; New Madrid County, Missouri, 1938*

153. Evans. *Interior of a general store; Moundville, Alabama, 1935*

154. Delano. *One of the area's oldest residents; Erin, New York, 1940*

155. Lange. *Sharecropper woman wearing black beads to remedy heart trouble; Hinds County, Mississippi, 1937*

156. Rothstein. *Farmer's wife; near Kearney, Nebraska, 1936*

157. Lange. *County courthouse just before primary election; Waco, Texas, 1938*

158. Lee. *Harlingen, Texas, 1939*

159. Evans. *Butcher shop sign; Mississippi, 1936*

160. Post Wolcott. *Transportation for "hep cats;" Louisville, Kentucky, 1940*

168. Lee. *Square dancing at home; Pie Town, New Mexico, 1940*

169. Lee. *Lafayette, Louisiana, 1938*

170. Lee. *Scrub-up time for a lumberjack; Minnesota, 1937*

171. Lee. *Sideshow at the State Fair; Donaldsonville, Louisiana, 1938*

172. Lee. *Lunchtime at an all-day community sing; Pie Town, New Mexico, 1940*

173. Lee. *Exploring the wonderful world of the mail-order catalogue; North Dakota, 1937*

174. Delano. *Laughter in a tobacco shed; Connecticut, 1940*

175. Shahn. *Wife and child of sharecropper; Ozark Mountains, Arkansas, 1935*

176. Lange. *Speaker at Steinbeck conference on agricultural organization—"Brother, it's pick 75¢ cotton or starve"; Bakersfield, California, 1938*

172

177. Lange. *Drought-stricken farmers on the shady side of town street while their crops burn up in the fields; Sallisaw, Oklahoma, 1936*

178. Shahn. *Sharecropper's wife and children; Boone County, Arkansas, 1935*

179. Lee. *Scene in agricultural workers' shack town; Oklahoma, 1939*

180. Rothstein. *Sharecropper's wife and child; Arkansas, 1938*

181. Lange. *Street meeting; San Francisco, California*

182. Post Wolcott. *Behind the bar; Birney, Montana, 1941*

183. Lange. *Tractored-out Texan who has become a migratory worker; Kern County, California, 1938*

184. Rothstein. *Fleeing a dust storm; Cimarron County, Oklahoma, 1936*

185. (overleaf) Post Wolcott. *Marion, Virginia, 1940*

Emphasize the idea of abundance—the "horn of plenty"—
and pour maple syrup over it . . .
I know your damned photographer's soul writhes, but . . .
Do you think I give a damn about a photographer's soul
with Hitler at our doorstep?

186. and 187. Delano. *Thanksgiving Day; Ledyard, Connecticut, 1940*

Dignity versus despair . . .
I believe that dignity wins out.

188. Lange. *Greek migratory woman living in cotton camp; Exeter, California, 1936*

189. Lee. *Former sharecropper; New Madrid, Missouri, 1938*

Selected Shooting Scripts

From R. E. Stryker
To all photographers

**Suggestions recently made by Robert Lynd
(co-author of *Middletown*)
for things which should be
photographed as American Background.**

FSA
1936

Home in the evening

Photographs showing the various ways that different income groups spend their evenings, for example:

Informal clothes

Listening to the radio

Bridge

More precise dress

Guests

Attending church

Follow through a set of pictures showing people on their way from their home to church

Getting out of church

Visiting and talking

Returning from church to home

Visiting and talking in the vestibule

Here again, note the difference in the habits of the various income groups.

The group activities of various income levels

The organized and unorganized activities of the various income groups

"Where can people meet?"

Well-to-do

Country clubs

Homes

Lodges

Poor

Beer halls

Pool halls

Saloons

Street corners

Garages

Cigar stores

Consider the same problem as applied to women.

Do women have as many meeting places as men?

It is probable that the women in the lower-income levels have far less opportunity of mingling with other women than do the women of the higher-income groups.

"How many people do you know?"

There is a marked difference here between the circle of acquaintanceship between the income groups and also on the basis of urban versus rural.

Backyards

"What do you see out of the kitchen window?"

Various exhibit pictures could be taken in different towns and on the basis of different income groups.

"Looking down my street"

Here again, a most interesting set of pictures could be taken, keeping in mind different income groups and different geographical areas.

People on and off the job.

How much different do people look and act when they are on the job than when they are off?

This would necessitate some very careful camera studies.

Pictures showing relationship between time and the job.

This would include such things as pictures taken of the same people every ten years, showing how people age in their work, and pictures emphasizing the aged man and woman and the job.

The effect of the depression in the smaller towns of the United States.

To include such things as the growth of small independent shops, stores, and businesses in the small towns; for example, the store opened up on the sun porch, the beauty shop in the living room

The baseball diamond as an important part of our general landscape.

This is particularly noticeable when one views small towns from the air.

"Fit for the likes of us"

What are the things which we feel comfortable doing with some and not with others?

Relationship between density of population and income of such things as

Pressed clothes

Polished shoes and so on

Is it likely in large industrial areas that even the poor groups will make a greater effort to have polished shoes, pressed clothes, than the same or even a higher-income group might in the smaller populated areas. What effect does wealth have on this?

"How do people look?"

In towns of various sizes—1500, 25,000 to 30,000, 100,000. Consider the same thing from a geographical standpoint.

The wall decorations in homes as an index to the different income groups and their reactions.

The photographic study of the difference in the men's world and the women's world.

A photographic study of use of leisure time in various income groups.

Compare headlines regionally.

Take the same topics such as a kidnapping or other news item with national interest and note the manner in which it is treated in the different parts of the country.

From R. E. Stryker
To Russell Lee,
Arthur Rothstein,
in particular

I. Production of foods—fruits, vegetables, meat, poultry, eggs, milk and milk products, miscellaneous products.

a. Packaging and processing of above

b. Picking, hauling, sorting, preparing, drying, canning, packaging, loading for shipping

c. Field operations—planting; cultivation; spraying

d. Dramatic pictures of fields, show "pattern" of the country; get feeling of the productive earth, boundless acres.

e. Warehouses filled with food, raw and processed, cans, boxes, bags, etc.

II. Poultry—large-scale operations

Hatching, shipping chicks

Get a few pictures "cute" of little chicks

Real close-ups

Eggs—get "pictorial" shots of eggs in baskets, in piles, in crates (get pattern pictures for posters)

Dressed poultry

Chickens in pens and yards

Feeding operations

III. General farming — get pictures of representative small farms (California — Texas) General farming, buildings, farmer & family, farmer at work.

IV. Small town under war conditions

Select a small town some distance from large cities and make a camera study of how this town looks under war conditions.

Civilian Defense Activities

Meetings of all kinds—Red Cross

Farm groups, etc.

Look for a town near an Army Camp

Signs—stores, filling stations, etc.

Selective Service

Registration of new age groups

Home gardens, Civilian Defense Activities

Schools. More neighborliness (Any evidence of this?)

V. Auto and auto tire rationing. A civilian population gets off rubber tires. (Many things should be photographed now before disappearance or marked decline.)

Old tires piles.

Used car lots. Especially when enormous numbers of cars are stored.

Signs—any sign which suggests rubber (or other commodity) shortage, rationing, etc. Horse-drawn vehicles. Blacksmith shops, harness shops, buggies, delivery wagons, horse drays (for trucks), bicycles.

(What will happen to roadside hamburger stand?) Watch for closed filling stations or eat joints.

VI. The highway

Watch for any signs which indicate a country at war.

"Man at Work" pictures. We are still short of these pictures. These should include:

(1) highway building—big stuff, e.g., in the Rocky Mts. or major highways.

(2) Repair and maintenance.

(3) Emphasize the men.

VII. (for R. Lee) Mining, California, Arizona, New Mexico

Get pictures showing increased activities among prospective and small operating outfits.

Mercury—near San Jose, California. Cement, Kaiser's cement plant near San Jose, California.

(See Jack Tolan. Also Sat. Eve. Post article on Kaiser.)

Miners—faces & miners at work

VIII. The land

The long shots for a "feel" of the country

Details

IX. People—*we must have at once*:

Pictures of men, women and children who appear as if they really believed in the U.S. Get people with a little spirit. Too many in our file now paint the U.S. as an old person's home and that just about everyone is too old to work and too malnourished to care much what happens. (Don't misunderstand the above. FSA is still interested in the lower-income groups and we want to continue to photograph this group.) We particularly need young men and women who work in our factories, the young men who build our bridges, roads, dams and large factories.

Housewives in their kitchen or in the yard picking flowers.

More contented-looking old couples—woman sewing, man reading; sitting on porch; working in garden; sitting in park; coming from church; at picnics, at meetings.

Bibliography

ARCHIVES

Farm Security Administration Collection. Prints and Photographs Division, Library of Congress. Contains the most complete set of FSA photographs. Pictures available to the public at a cost of $2.50 per 8 x 10 glossy print.

Farm Security Administration File, Social and Economic Records Division and National Archives Records Service, Washington, D.C.

Stryker, Roy, Collection, University of Louisville Photographic Archive. Contains the largest number of letters and clippings relating to the Farm Security Administration Historical Section; also Stryker's picture collection, shooting scripts, personal books, letters, and memorabilia.

Stryker, Roy, Correspondence, Archives of American Art, Detroit. Includes a valuable series of interviews by Richard K. Doud.

SELECTED READINGS

Agee, James, and Evans, Walker. *Let Us Now Praise Famous Men.* New York, 1941.

Anderson, Sherwood. *Home Town: The Face of America.* New York, 1940.

Baldwin, Sidney. *Poverty and Politics: The Rise and Decline of the Farm Security Administration.* Chapel Hill, 1968.

Caldwell, Erskine, and Bourke-White, Margaret. *You Have Seen Their Faces.* New York, 1937.

Chamberlain, Samuel, ed. *Fair Is Our Land.* New York, 1942.

Collier, John, Jr. *Visual Anthropology: Photography as a Research Method.* New York, 1967.

Conkin, Paul. *Tomorrow a New World: The New Deal Community Program.* Ithaca, New York, 1959.

Conrad, David E. *The Forgotten Farmers: The Story of Sharecroppers in the New Deal.* Urbana, 1965.

Evans, Walker. *American Photographs.* New York, 1938.

First Annual Report of the Resettlement Administration. Washington, D.C. 1936.

Frank, Waldo, and others, eds. *America and Alfred Stieglitz: A Collective Portrait.* New York, 1934.

Garver, Thomas H., ed. *Just Before the War: Urban America as Seen by Photographers of the Farm Security Administration.* Boston, 1968.

Gutman, Judith Mara. *Lewis W. Hine and the American Social Conscience.* New York, 1968.

Hine, Lewis. *Men at Work: Photographic Studies of Modern Men and Machines.* New York, 1932.

Horan, James D. *Mathew Brady, Historian with a Camera.* New York, 1955.

Hurley, F. Jack. *Portrait of a Decade: Roy Stryker and the Development of Documentary Photography in the Thirties.* Baton Rouge, 1972.

Ickes, Harold L. *The Secret Diary of Harold L. Ickes,* 3 vols. New York, 1953.

Kirkendall, Richard S. *Social Scientists and Farm Politics in the Age of Roosevelt.* Columbia, Missouri, 1966.

Lange, Dorothea. *Dorothea Lange.* New York, 1966.

_____. *Dorothea Lange Looks at the American Country Woman.* Fort Worth, 1967.

_____, and Taylor, Paul Schuster. *An American Exodus: A Record of Human Erosion.* New York, 1939.

Leuchtenburg, William E. *Franklin D. Roosevelt and the New Deal.* New York, 1963.

Lynd, Robert S., and Lynd, Helen M. *Middletown: A study in American Culture.* New York, 1929.

MacLeish, Archibald. *Land of the Free.* New York, 1938.

McCamy, James L. *Government Publicity—Its Practice in Federal Administration.* Chicago, 1939.

Maddox, Jerald C. Introduction to *Walker Evans: Photographs for the Farm Security Administration, 1935–1938.* Forthcoming.

Moley, Raymond. *After Seven Years.* New York, 1939.

_____. *The First New Deal.* New York, 1966.

Newhall, Beaumont. *The History of Photography.* New York, rev. ed. 1970. Also available in paperback.

Nixon, Herman Clarence. *Forty Acres and Steel Mules.* Chapel Hill, 1938.

Odum, Howard. *Southern Regions of the United States.* Chapel Hill, 1936.

Pollack, Peter. *The Picture History of Photography.* New York, rev. ed. 1970.

Raper, Arthur F. *Preface to Peasantry: A Tale of Two Black Belt Counties.* Chapel Hill, 1936.

_____, with F.S.A.; photographs by Jack Delano. *Tenants of the Almighty.* New York, 1943.

_____, and Reid, Ira DeA. *Sharecroppers All.* Chapel Hill, 1941.

Riis, Jacob. *How the Other Half Lives.* New York, 1890.

_____. *The Making of an American.* New York, 1901.

Rodman, Selden. *Portrait of the Artist as an American, Ben Shahn: A Biography with Pictures.* New York, 1949.

Roosevelt, Eleanor. *This I Remember.* New York, 1949.

Schlesinger, A. M., Jr. *The Age of Roosevelt: The Crisis of the Old Order, 1919–1933.* Cambridge, 1957.

Smith, J. Russell. *North America.* New York, 1925.

Steichen, Edward, ed. *The Bitter Years, 1935–1941: Rural America As Seen by the Photographers of the Farm Security Administration.* New York, 1962.

_____, ed. *The Family of Man.* New York, 1955.

Sternsher, Bernard. *Rexford Tugwell and the New Deal.* New Brunswick, 1964.

Taft, Robert. *Photography and the American Scene, A Social History, 1839–1889.* New York, 1938.

Tugwell, Rexford G. *The Brains Trust.* New York, 1968.

_____. *The Democratic Roosevelt: A Biography of Franklin D. Roosevelt.* New York, 1957.

_____. *The Stricken Land.* Garden City, New York, 1947.

_____; Munro, Thomas; and Stryker, Roy E. *American Economic Life.* New York, 1925.

U.S.D.A. *Yearbook of Agriculture, 1940: Farmers in a Changing World.* Washington, D.C., 1940.

Vance, Rupert B. *How the Other Half Is Housed: A Pictorial Record of Sub-Minimum Farm Housing in the South.* Chapel Hill, 1936.

Weiss, Margaret R., ed. *Ben Shahn, Photographer.* New York, 1973.

Wright, Richard, and Rosskam, Edwin. *Twelve Million Black Voices: A Folk History of the Negro in the United States.* New York. 1941.

Acknowledgments

A book of this magnitude is the result of the effort and love of many people. The authors thank the staff of the University of Louisville Photographic Archive for hours of research and particularly for lending dozens of prints from the Stryker collection. We are especially indebted to Robert J. Doherty, Jr., John W. Church, and James C. Anderson, all of the University of Louisville, for their help and understanding. At the Library of Congress we have been fortunate in gaining the assistance of Leroy Bellamy, Curator of the Prints and Photographs Division and a master of the FSA Collection. Dr. Alan Fern, Assistant Chief of the Prints and Photographs Division, Dr. Edgar Breitenbach, Chief of the Prints and Photographs Division, William Younger, Robert Overmiller, and the skilled craftsmen at the lab of the Library of Congress are all deserving of our deepest gratitude. To Phyllis Stryker Wilson we are especially indebted for fine meals, good company, endless errands, and keeping the coffee ready.

Nancy Wood offers her particular thanks to Patricia Lambdin Moore, her editor at the New York Graphic Society, who bestowed upon this book her particular genius. And to typist Helen Lynch go thanks and a promise of new eyeglasses if not an easier manuscript next time. James Craig, of New York City, is warmly commended for his sensitive approach to the book's design.

Finally, F. Jack Hurley must be acknowledged for his fundamental contribution to the literature on the FSA photographs: *Portrait of a Decade: Roy Stryker and the Development of Documentary Photography in the Thirties,* Baton Rouge, 1972.

Photographic Notes

Print Sources

Photographic prints used for reproduction in the manufacture of this book have been obtained from the following:

Library of Congress, Washington, D.C.—V, VI, 1, 3, 4, 7, 10, 12, 13, 14, 15, 16, 19, 20, 22, 23, 26, 27, 28, 29, 30, 31, 32, 33, 34, 35, 36, 37, 38, 40, 41, 47, 48, 49, 50, 52, 55, 56, 58, 59, 60, 61, 63, 64, 65, 66, 67, 68, 69, 70, 71, 72, 73, 75, 76, 77, 78, 79, 80, 81, 82, 83, 84, 86, 87, 88, 91, 92, 93, 94, 95, 96, 97, 98, 99, 102, 103, 104, 105, 106, 107, 110, 113, 114, 115, 119, 120, 121, 122, 123, 124, 125, 126, 128, 129, 130, 131, 132, 133, 135, 136, 137, 140, 142, 143, 144, 145, 146, 147, 151, 153, 154, 156, 158, 160, 162, 163, 165, 166, 168, 170, 172, 174, 175, 176, 177, 178, 180, 182

Roy Stryker's Personal Collection, Grand Junction, Colorado — II, III, IV, VII, 2, 5, 9, 11, 17, 18, 21, 24, 42, 45, 51, 53, 57, 62, 85, 90, 108, 109, 112, 116, 118, 127, 134, 148, 149, 150, 155, 161, 167, 171, 173, 179, 180, 181, 183, 184, 187

Roy Stryker Collection, Photographic Archive, University of Louisville, Kentucky—VIII, 6, 8, 25, 39, 43, 44, 46, 54, 74, 89, 100, 101, 111, 117, 138, 139, 141, 152, 157, 159, 164, 169, 185, 186, 188, 189

Arthur Rothstein—IX

Photographic Credits

Roman numerals refer to the FSA pictures accompanying the text (pp. 7–20).

Bubley, Esther, 28

Carter, Paul, 79

Collier, John, Jr., 142

Collins, Marjory, 45, 49

Delano, Jack, VI, 11, 23, 25, 29, 50, 53, 54, 59, 71, 91, 108, 109, 112, 136, 139, 141, 154, 162, 174, 186, 187

Evans, Walker, 43, 51, 81, 99, 105, 115, 120, 122, 126, 128, 131, 153, 159

Lange, Dorothea, IX, 2, 5, 20, 35, 40, 41, 48, 60, 77, 78, 80, 82, 85, 90, 92, 93, 95, 121, 124, 125, 137, 144, 155, 157, 167, 176, 177, 181, 183, 188

Lee, Russell, IV, VII, VIII, 6, 7, 9, 10, 12, 14, 17, 18, 24, 27, 30, 31, 32, 36, 39, 46, 55, 57, 62, 64, 67, 69, 73, 76, 84, 87, 97, 98, 100, 110, 127, 129, 130, 138, 140, 143, 147, 149, 151, 152, 158, 161, 168, 169, 170, 171, 172, 173, 179, 189

Mydans, Carl, 58

Post Wolcott, Marion, 3, 16, 19, 38, 63, 65, 68, 70, 86, 89, 107, 117, 133, 145, 150, 160, 164, 166, 182, 185

Rothstein, Arthur, II, III, V, 1, 22, 37, 42, 44, 61, 66, 74, 83, 94, 96, 101, 102, 103, 104, 111, 135, 146, 148, 156, 180, 184

Shahn, Ben, 8, 15, 26, 33, 34, 114, 116, 118, 119, 123, 138, 175, 178

Vachon, John, 4, 13, 21, 47, 52, 56, 72, 75, 88, 106, 113, 132, 134, 163, 165

Library of Congress Negative Numbers

Copies of the FSA prints in this book may be purchased from: Prints and Photographs Division, The Library of Congress, Washington, D.C. 20540. The purchase order for a particular print should include its negative number and, as a secondary aid, its caption.

II. LC-USF34-28371-D
III. LC-USF34-28370-D
IV. LC-USF34-33125-D
V. LC-USF33-2679-M4
VI. LC-USF33-45295-D
VII. LC-USF34-12010-M4
VIII. LC-USF33-11789-M3
IX. LC-USF34-9058-C
1. LC-USF34-26116-D
2. LC-USF34-18660-C
3. LC-USF34-50720-E
4. LC-USF34-60713-D
5. LC-USF34-9328
6. LC-USZ62-10582
7. LC-USF33-11961-M1
8. LC-USF33-6121-M3
9. LC-USF33-11785-M1
10. LC-USF33-11887-M1
11. LC-USF34-44563-D
12. LC-USF34-39130
13. LC-USF34-64475-D
14. LC-USF34-32053-D
15. LC-USF33-6628-M5
16. LC-USF33-31080-M5
17. LC-USF33-11554-M3
18. LC-USF34-36542
19. LC-USF34-57465-E
20. LC-USF34-17335-C
21. LC-USF34-60331
22. LC-USF33-2649-M5
23. LC-USF34-41124-E
24. LC-USF34-33034
25. LC-USF342-42180-A
26. LC-USF33-6258-M3
27. LC-USF342-30539-A
28. LC-USW3-29832
29. LC-USF34-46543-D
30. LC-USF33-11528-M2
31. LC-USF33-11272-M5
32. LC-USF33-12463-M2
33. LC-USF33-6130-M1
34. LC-USF33-6174-M3
35. LC-USF34-9860-C
36. LC-USF34-36620-D
37. LC-USF33-2325-M3
38. LC-USF33-30341-M3
39. LC-USF33-11151-M5
40. LC-USF34-17079-C
41. LC-USF34-21235
42. LC-USF34-25956
43. LC-USF342-8140-A
44. LC-USF33-2173-M1
45. LC-USW3-11705
46. LC-USF33-11783-M5
47. LC-USF34-64470-D
48. LC-USW3-9599
49. LC-USW3-10954-E
50. LC-USF34-42858-D
51. LC-USF342-1167-A
52. LC-USF34-60037-D
53. LC-USF34-46508-D
54. LC-USW3-16951
55. LC-USF33-12484-M2
56. LC-USW3-10815
57. LC-USF34-71171
58. LC-USF34-6322-D
59. LC-USF34-41294
60. LC-USF34-16208-E
61. LC-USF33-2866-M1
62. LC-USF34-35456-D
63. LC-USF33-30180-M2
64. LC-USF34-32010-D
65. LC-USF33-31161-M1
66. LC-USF34-26868-D
67. LC-USF34-30587
68. LC-USF34-54368-D
69. LC-USF34-36930
70. LC-USF34-52594-D
71. LC-USF34-43997-D
72. LC-USF33-1368-M1
73. LC-USF33-13095-M2
74. LC-USF34-0427-D
75. LC-USF34-61043
76. LC-USF34-33417-D
77. LC-USF34-9745-E
78. LC-USF34-16239-C
79. LC-USF341-2841-B
80. LC-USF34-9666
81. LC-USF34-8138
82. LC-USF34-19480-C
83. LC-USF34-5008-D
84. LC-USF34-37420-D
85. LC-USF34-18401
86. LC-USF34-55240-D
87. LC-USF33-11702-M5
88. LC-USF34-61720
89. LC-USF34-57526
90. LC-USF34-16317
91. LC-USF34-45718
92. LC-USF34-18280
93. LC-USZ62-19804
94. LC-USF34-1128-C
95. LC-USF34-16237
96. LC-USF34-29412
97. LC-USF34-30968
98. LC-USF33-11896-M4
99. LC-USF342-8133-A
100. LC-USF33-11602-M5
101. LC-USF34-29143
102. LC-USF34-25121
103. LC-USF34-5553-E
104. LC-USF34-29162-D
105. LC-USF342-8159-A
106. LC-USF34-64221-D
107. LC-USF34-55707-D
108. LC-USF34-44638-D
109. LC-USF34-40682-D
110. LC-USF34-34340-D
111. LC-USF33-2590-M1
112. LC-USF34-41577-D
113. LC-USF34-64805-D
114. LC-USF33-6611-M1
115. LC-USF342-1295-A
116. LC-USF33-6093-M5
117. LC-USF34-53121
118. LC-USF33-6478-M1
119. LC-USF33-6204-M1
120. LC-USF34-8213-C
121. LC-USF34-18258-C
122. LC-USF342-8057-A
123. LC-USF33-6543-M1
124. LC-USF34-9625
125. LC-USF34-18300-E
126. LC-USF342-8010-A
127. LC-USF34-34404
128. LC-USF342-1164-A
129. LC-USF33-11864-M3
130. LC-USF34-33418-D
131. LC-USF33-6717-M3
132. LC-USF34-61897
133. LC-USF34-51274-D
134. LC-USF34-62066-D
135. LC-USF34-420-D
136. LC-USF34-40540
137. LC-USF34-18216-E
138. LC-USF33-6023-M4
139. LC-USF34-43863
140. LC-USF34-38814-D
141. LC-USF34-46288-D
142. LC-USW3-15206-C
143. LC-USF34-31938
144. LC-USF34-21993-C
145. LC-USF34-55314-D
146. LC-USF34-26161-D
147. LC-USF34-33421-D
148. LC-USF34-24196
149. LC-USF34-32264
150. LC-USF34-50348-E
151. LC-USF34-31221
152. LC-USF33-11438-M2
153. LC-USF34-8164-A
154. LC-USF34-41443-D
155. LC-USF34-17112-C
156. LC-USF34-4405-E
157. LC-USF34-18261-C
158. LC-USF34-32188
159. LC-USF342-8096-A
160. LC-USF34-55322-D
161. LC-USF33-12344-M1
162. LC-USF34-44600-D
163. LC-USF34-8522
164. LC-USF34-30539
165. LC-USF34-65507-D
166. LC-USF34-52487-D
167. LC-USF34-20017
168. LC-USF34-36912
169. LC-USF33-11862-M4
170. LC-USF34-30689
171. LC-USF33-11770-M3
172. LC-USF33-12786-M1
173. LC-USF34-30439
174. LC-USF34-41573
175. LC-USF33-6032-M1
176. LC-USF34-18774-D
177. LC-USF34-9669-E
178. LC-USF33-6035-M4
179. LC-USF34-34006-D
180. LC-USF33-2022-M3
181. LC-USF34-9727
182. LC-USF34-58504-D
183. LC-USF34-18607
184. LC-USF34-4052-E
185. LC-USF34-56104
186. LC-USF34-42424
187. LC-USF34-42712
188. LC-USF34-9866-C
189. LC-USF33-11442-M2